D0900280

EXPLORE
COLONIAL
AMERICA

THE FIRST
THANKSGIVING

Sarah Gilman

Enslow Publishing
101 W. 23rd Street
Suite 240
New York, NY 10011
USA

enslow.com

Published in 2017 by Enslow Publishing, LLC.
101 W. 23rd Street, Suite 240, New York, NY 10011

Library of Congress Cataloging-in-Publication Data

Names: Gilman, Sarah, author.
Title: The first Thanksgiving / Sarah Gilman.
Description: New York, NY : Enslow Publishing, [2017] | Series: Explore colonial America | Includes bibliographical references and index. |Audience: Grades 4-6.
Identifiers: LCCN 2015047558| ISBN 9780766078697 (library bound) | ISBN 9780766078758 (pbk.) | ISBN 9780766078574 (6-pack)
Subjects: LCSH: Massachusetts--History--New Plymouth, 1620-1691--Juvenile literature. | Pilgrims (New Plymouth Colony)--Juvenile literature. | Wampanoag Indians--Juvenile literature. | Thanksgiving Day--Juvenile literature.
Classification: LCC F68 .G54 2006 | DDC 974.402--dc23
LC record available at http://lccn.loc.gov/2015047558

To Our Readers: We have done our best to make sure all website addresses in this book were active and appropriate when we went to press. However, the author and the publisher have no control over and assume no liability for the material available on those websites or on any websites they may link to. Any comments or suggestions can be sent by e-mail to customerservice@enslow.com.

Portions of this book originally appeared in the book *Celebrate the First Thanksgiving* by Elaine Landau.

Photo Credits: Throughout book: javarman/Shutterstock.com (tan background), STILLFX/Shutterstock.com (American flag background), Peliken/Shutterstock.com (white stars on blue background); cover, p. 1 Everett Historical/Shutterstock.com; pp. 4, 6, 7, 17, 18, 21, 25, 31, 35 © North Wind Picture Archives; p. 6 Kean Collection/Archive Photos/Getty Images; p. 9 Robert W. Weir, photograph courtesy Architect of the Capitol/ File:Embarkation of the Pilgrims.jpg/Wikimedia Commons; p. 12 Harold M. Lambert/Kean Collection/Archive Photos/Getty Images; p. 14 Library of Congress/File:The Mayflower Compact 1620 cph.3g07155.jpg/Wikimedia Commons; p. 23 Ed Vebell/Getty Images; p. 26 Melanie Stetson Freeman/The Christian Science Monitor via Getty Images; p. 29 Archive Photos/Getty Images; p. 34 Kean Collection/Getty Images; p. 37 Library of Congress/File:The First Thanksgiving cph.3g04961.jpg/Wikimedia Commons: p. 40 monkeybusinessimages/iStock/Thinkstock.com; p. 42 Library of Congress; p. 43 Superstock/Getty Images.

CONTENTS

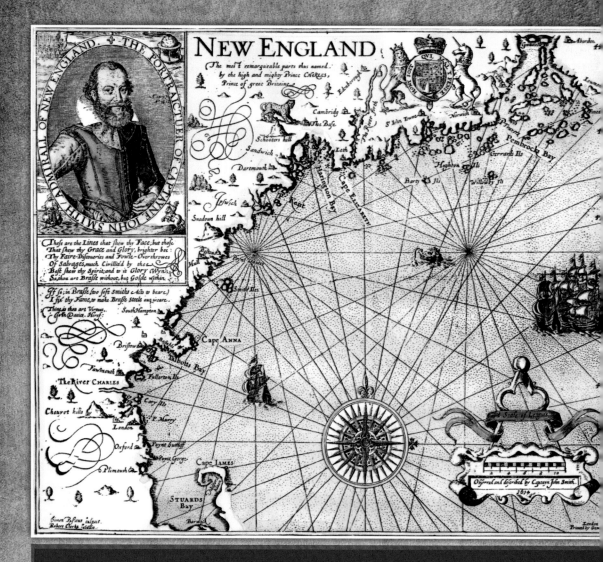

The harvest feast that we recognize as the first Thanksgiving took place off the coast of Massachusetts, where Pilgrims settled among the local American Indians.

THE WAMPANOAG INDIANS

The Pilgrims were not the first people to settle in America. American Indians lived there earlier. Among them was a group we know as the Wampanoag. They mostly lived along the shores of Massachusetts and on nearby islands.

The Wampanoag were peaceful people who farmed, fished, and hunted. Family ties were strong among them. Both the old and the young were well-cared for.

EUROPEANS ARRIVE

The Wampanoag had never seen a European until the 1500s. That was when explorers, fishermen, and traders began arriving. They did not stay in North America long. Yet, they left behind diseases from Europe.

The Wampanoag Indians moved around the region as the seasons changed. Their women grew corn, beans, and squash. Their men hunted game and fished.

Often, these diseases were deadly to American Indians. Their bodies were not used to them. Sometimes disease wiped out whole villages.

That happened to the Patuxet Indians. The Patuxet were close relatives of the Wampanoag and had lived nearby. Nearly every person in the Patuxet village died from a disease that may have been smallpox. The few who lived went to stay with the Wampanoag.

American Indians had no immunity to the strange diseases brought by Europeans to the New World. As a result, many of their population was wiped out in time.

By the early 1600s, more Europeans came to North America. Now they brought their families. They also brought guns and ammunition. These Europeans had come to stay in America.

The settlers wanted the American Indians out of the way. They wanted to take their land. In time, the American Indians feared for both their land and their lives.

7

THE PILGRIMS SET SAIL

The *Mayflower* set sail from Plymouth, England, on September 6, 1620. Inside the 100-foot (30-meter) wooden ship, 102 passengers were starting an exciting journey. They were leaving England to start a new life in North America.

Crossing the Atlantic would take about two months. At first, the weather was mild. But those pleasant days gave way to powerful storms. Fierce winds and high waves tossed the vessel about on the ocean.

A DIFFICULT VOYAGE

The stormy weather was very hard on the passengers. Many became extremely seasick. Some of them found it hard to stand. Some passengers remained below deck for most of

The Pilgrims hit some bad weather on their journey. The storms made the seas very rough. One of the Pilgrims fell overboard. Luckily, he clung to the ropes on the ship's side. The crew pulled him up to safety.

the voyage. That area was usually used to carry cargo. Now it held people as well as the farm animals taken on the journey.

A large number of the Pilgrims could not even keep their food down. Not that there was much to eat anyway. The passengers had some salted pork, beef, and dried codfish. All the cheese had gone moldy. Maggots and rats had gotten into the hard biscuits and dried peas.

Some on board became quite ill. Before the trip was over, two people on the *Mayflower* died. One was a passenger and the other a sailor.

Later on, strong winds caused a beam on the main deck to crack. If it were not repaired, the ship could develop a serious leak. This scared some of the passengers and crew. Several wanted to turn back. However, it was soon fixed and the *Mayflower* stayed on course.

There were some joyful moments, too. During the voyage, a woman named Elizabeth Hopkins gave birth. She and her husband, Stephen, gave their new son a fitting name. The boy was called Oceanus.

CHAPTER THREE

THE NEW WORLD

On November 9, 1620, the passengers on the *Mayflower* spotted land. Their journey had taken two months. They had arrived at the tip of the area now known as Cape Cod, Massachusetts. The passengers hugged one another and celebrated. Some dropped to their knees to give thanks.

The *Mayflower* passengers had not had enough money for their voyage. A group of businessmen had paid for it. However, the trip was not a gift. The settlers would have to pay them back. They were to do so with furs, fish, and lumber from North America.

No one knew if these Pilgrims could build a thriving colony. Some on board had their doubts. The *Mayflower* passengers did not always get along.

The Pilgrims finally touched the land of the New World after a long and difficult journey. However, they had been thrown off course and landed in New England instead of New York.

WHO WERE THE PILGRIMS?

Forty-six of them had left England for religious reasons. These were known as Separatists. The Separatists had separated from the Church of England. They wanted to worship in their own way and felt unable to do this in England. Now they hoped to start a colony in North America where they could worship as they pleased.

The Separatists that came to New England called themselves Saints. Not all the *Mayflower* passengers were Saints. The Saints called the others on board Strangers. The Strangers were not coming to North America for religious reasons. They came to build a better life for themselves. Some hoped to become wealthy.

Today, we call both the Saints and the Strangers Pilgrims. However, a "pilgrim" is someone taking a religious journey. This was not true of all the *Mayflower* passengers.

The Saints did not quite trust the Strangers. The Strangers did not care for the Saints either. They did not like the Saints telling them how they should live their lives. Nevertheless, both groups would have to live together in North America.

EXPLORE THE FACTS

PILGRIM CLOTHING

We think of the Pilgrims in black-and-white costumes. But they only wore black and white on Sundays and special occasions. On other days, they wore colorful clothing. Until the age of eight, both boys and girls wore dresses!

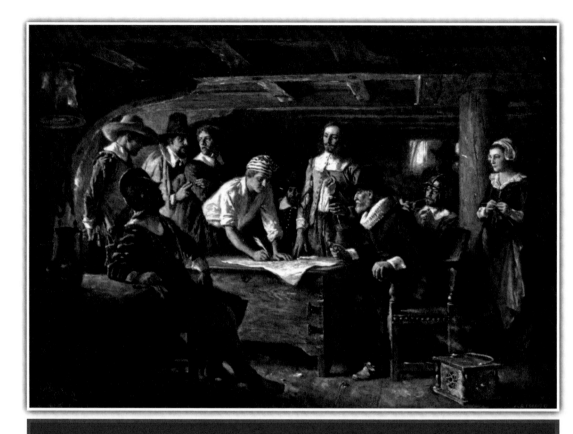

Since things were not going according to plan, the passengers drew up the Mayflower Compact. They also elected John Carver to lead the colony.

THE MAYFLOWER COMPACT

They had made an arrangement with the Virginia Company of London to start a colony in the area known as present-day New York State. The Virginia Company needed more settlers in North America. Its first colony in Jamestown, Virginia, was not doing well.

But now, some things would need to be worked out. The storms had thrown the ship off course. The Virginia Company did not control the territory this far north. Settling on uncharted land worried some on the *Mayflower*. Would everyone still follow the terms of the original agreement?

To make sure they did, the *Mayflower* passengers drew up their own agreement. It would later be called the Mayflower Compact.

On November 11, 1620, both Saints and Strangers signed the Mayflower Compact. Through it, they agreed to pass laws and elect officials. This helped start an important tradition in American government—the direct election of our leaders.

Before leaving the ship, a Saint named John Carver was elected governor of their colony. Carver was a successful businessman. He was also known to be fair.

Everyone felt better after signing an agreement. Yet no one could be sure how things would really turn out. Now they could only work hard and hope for the best.

CHAPTER FOUR

ONCE ASHORE

The *Mayflower* passengers were happy to end their difficult voyage. But they did not know what they would find in the New World. On November 11, a group of sixteen men went ashore while the others stayed on the boat. They later returned safely with firewood. Two days later, all the passengers left the *Mayflower*. The children played on the beach while the women washed clothes. Some of the men went exploring.

EVIDENCE OF INDIANS

The Pilgrims worried about American Indians in the area. They soon found some empty wigwams. These were round-roofed houses that belonged to the Wampanoag Indians. The Pilgrims took whatever they pleased from these. They carried out food, tools, blankets, and baskets.

They also found the American Indians' supply of dried corn. The Wampanoag had buried it in the ground. The Pilgrims dug

The Pilgrims were aware that they would be settling among local American Indians. Still, they did not know what to expect from their new neighbors.

The Pilgrims soon determined that the place where they had landed would not be a good location for a colony. After some exploration, they sailed to the present-day site of Plymouth.

it up and took it with them. They did not see this as wrong. This was partly because they did not respect the Indians. They wrongly believed that American Indians were savages. They also thought that God had put these supplies in their path so they could take them. However, when they finally met the owners of the corn later, they paid them for what they took.

IN SEARCH OF A PLACE TO SETTLE

The *Mayflower* settlers did not remain at Cape Cod for long. It was not the best place to settle. There was no source of fresh water in sight. Some settlers also became ill after eating the mussels they found on the shore.

The Pilgrims had a smaller boat with them on the *Mayflower*. This vessel could sail safely in shallow waters. An exploring party of eighteen men was formed. They sailed out to see the broader area. Among those who went were Governor Carver, another Saint named William Bradford, and Captain Miles Standish, a military man. On December 8, 1620, these men spotted some American Indians and exchanged shots with them. The spot on Cape Cod where this took place came to be known as "the First Encounter."

The Pilgrims continued to look for a good place for the colony. Then on December 11, the men found the perfect spot for a new colony. It was the area that we know today as Plymouth, Massachusetts. The Pilgrims found fresh water there. There were cleared fields in which to plant crops. This site even had a hill where Captain Miles Standish could build a fort for defense. The Pilgrims felt that they could make their new home there.

A NEW HOME

On December 16, the *Mayflower* passengers joined the exploring party. When they arrived in Plymouth, the weather was growing colder and there had already been some heavy snows.

The new settlers needed to build shelters. There was no time to waste. They cut down some trees to quickly build shelters. The men also built a palisade, or barrier of logs around the village. This was done for protection.

MYSTERIOUS NEIGHBORS

The new settlers had worried about Indian attacks. Even before leaving England, they had heard about attacks on the Jamestown colony. They had also briefly battled with the Indians during "the First Encounter" on Cape Cod. However, so far, no American Indians had come to their settlement.

The first order of business, aside from finding food for sustenance, was to build shelters. The Pilgrims worked very hard to build homes and a wall of defense from possible Indian attack.

The Pilgrims had hired Miles Standish in England to serve as their military adviser. Standish was very concerned about threats from Indians and also from wild animals.

EXPLORE THE FACTS

A FORT

Miles Standish built a fort on top of a hill. This was a strategic lookout. From there, he could see the surrounding woods and the settlement of Plymouth. He also could spot any ships approaching from the ocean.

Yet, the Pilgrims never felt safe. There were wolves in the surrounding woods. Sometimes they could be heard howling at night.

In the distance, the Pilgrims also often saw smoke. It came from American Indian campfires. Now and then a settler would see an American Indian in the woods. The Pilgrims did not know what to expect.

Later, they learned more about their Wampanoag neighbors. The spot the Pilgrims picked for their colony was well-known to these American Indians. It was once a Patuxet Indian village.

That was the reason why the Pilgrims had found cleared fields there. The Patuxet Indians had used these to plant corn. Now the Pilgrims would try to plant their crops there.

THE DEADLY WINTER

Between the long voyage and the lack of nutrition, many Pilgrims arrived in the New World weak and tired. Before long, some settlers became very ill.

SCURVY AND TYPHUS

A number of them developed a disease called scurvy. This comes from not getting enough Vitamin C. This vitamin is commonly found in fresh fruits and vegetables. Such foods were scarce on the voyage.

The Pilgrims with scurvy suffered. Their gums bled and their teeth fell out. Their joints ached and they always felt weak.

Some of the settlers probably also had typhus, another deadly disease. These Pilgrims ran high fevers. They had headaches and chills. Some had a rash that covered much of their body. The Pilgrims called their illnesses "the General Sickness."

Suffering from poor nutrition, an unforgiving climate, and over-whelming hard work, the settlement was plagued by illness. With few resources, there was not much that could be done.

They tried to nurse their loved ones back to health. But many people grew weaker each day. As the weeks passed, large numbers of them died. There was little time to mourn. They had to bury their dead to prevent more disease.

This was often done at night. The Pilgrims knew that the American Indians were watching them. They were still afraid of being attacked. They did not want the Indians to know how few settlers were left.

The Pilgrims who were not fortunate enough to survive that brutal winter were laid to rest on Burial Hill. This was also the site of Plymouth Colony's fort.

EXPLORE THE FACTS

BEER

The Pilgrims did not have much fresh water when they sailed to the New World. Instead, they drank a steady supply of beer. Even the children drank it! The Pilgrims may have added pine and spruce needles to the beer to help prevent scurvy.

THE NEED FOR FOOD

Meanwhile, the Pilgrims still needed to learn a great deal. They had no idea where the best fishing spots were. They were not very skilled at tracking animals either. They also did not know what crops would grow best in the area's rocky soil.

As a result, there was little food. The Pilgrims tried to get by on what they could find. They lived on nuts from trees, and clams and mussels from the ocean, but there was never enough. Everyone was always hungry. As they grew weaker, it became harder for them to work.

By March 31, 1621, nearly half the settlers who came over on the *Mayflower* had died of sickness or starvation. The ship had not returned to England yet. Many of its crew had died as well. Almost every family had lost someone. People wondered how they could go on. Yet they found the courage to do so.

THE AMERICAN INDIANS APPEAR

The Pilgrims knew that they had American Indian neighbors, although they still hadn't been seen. Finally, on February 16, 1621, a settler saw about a dozen American Indians in the forest. He quickly ran back to the colony. He told the others that the American Indians might be on their way there.

The Pilgrims prepared for an attack. They brought a cannon from the *Mayflower* to the colony. Captain Standish formed a tiny fighting force of settlers.

SAMOSET

The Pilgrims were prepared for the worst. But none of the American Indians the settler saw ever came. Then on March 16,

After months of expecting the worst from the local American Indians, the Pilgrims were surprised when Samoset came by and welcomed them to the area.

1621, one American Indian walked into the colony. His name was Samoset.

Samoset appeared at the doorway of the Pilgrims' meetinghouse. The Pilgrims were shocked to see him standing there. They were even more surprised to hear him speak English.

Samoset had learned English from English fishermen. He had sailed with them along the Atlantic coast. Samoset told the Pilgrims about their neighbors—the Wampanoag Indians. He explained how they had lived in this area for many years. Samoset also spoke about a great Wampanoag chief named Massasoit.

Since it was getting late, Samoset spent the night with the Pilgrims. He stayed in the home of Elizabeth and Stephen Hopkins. The Hopkinses tried to make Samoset comfortable. He left the next morning in a very good mood.

EXPLORE THE FACTS

A MATRILINEAL SOCIETY

The Wampanoag Indians were matrilineal. This means that women controlled property in their society. Also, names and lineage passed through the women's side of the family. This was quite different from the way the Pilgrims' society was organized.

A HOPEFUL VISIT

The next day, Samoset returned to the colony. This time, he came with five other Wampanoag Indians. They brought beaver pelts (skins) for the settlers.

The Pilgrims were delighted with the pelts. They hoped the Wampanoag would begin trading with them. The settlers had brought trinkets and shiny knives to trade with the American Indians. The Pilgrims became hopeful. It looked like the Wampanoag would not be their enemy. Instead, they would help the colony survive.

American Indians had long traded pelts and other goods with European explorers. Now, the Wampanoag would trade with the colonists. The Pilgrims found this encouraging.

CHAPTER EIGHT

PEACE WITH THE WAMPANOAG

Samoset returned to the Pilgrim's colony on March 22. With him he brought an American Indian named Tisquantum. This new visitor also spoke English, and he would be a helpful resource to the Pilgrims.

SQUANTO'S STORY

Years ago, Tisquantum had been captured by an English sea captain. The captain took him to Europe. There Tisquantum was sold into slavery. He was given the nickname "Squanto." Somehow, Squanto was able to escape and return home on an English fishing ship.

However, he had a painful homecoming. Squanto was a Patuxet Indian. He returned to a village wiped out by disease. So he went to live with the Wampanoag.

32

TEACHING THE PILGRIMS

Now Squanto decided to help the Pilgrims. He stayed at the colony. He taught the Pilgrims everything they needed to know.

Squanto taught the Pilgrims new ways to fish. Squanto could catch eels with his feet. Before long, the Pilgrims were digging for clams. They set traps for lobsters, too. Having enough meat was important to the Pilgrims. So Squanto taught the men how to track and hunt animals.

By spring, it was time to plant crops. Squanto brought the Pilgrims seeds to grow corn, peas, squash, and beans. Squanto also showed the settlers which nuts, fruits, and berries were safe to eat. He even taught them how to use plants and herbs as medicines.

MASSASOIT AND THE PEACE TREATY

Through Squanto, the Pilgrims met Massasoit, a great Wampanoag chief. On March 23, 1621, Massasoit and the Pilgrims signed a peace treaty. The peace between them would last over fifty years.

EXPLORE THE FACTS

SQUANTO'S TIPS

Squanto showed the Pilgrims how to grow squash and beans. He taught them to put a dead fish in the soil with their seeds. The fish is a fertilizer and helps plants grow.

Squanto was instrumental in the Pilgrims' survival during their first year in the New World. Had the American Indians not taught them to fish, plant crops, and navigate the land, they likely would have died from starvation and poor nutrition.

Another good sign for the success of the colony was its relationship with the Wampanoag. This was sealed in a peace treaty, brokered by Chief Massasoit and John Carver.

On April 5, 1621, the *Mayflower* set sail for England. None of the colonists chose to leave with the ship. With Squanto's help, they were there to stay. However, they still had a lot of hard work to do over the summer. They had to do all they could to make sure they had plenty of food for the winter.

THE FIRST THANKSGIVING

A fter a terrible winter, the Pilgrims were delighted that the spring and summer of 1621 were successful. They had learned how to hunt and plant crops. By fall, they had had a good corn harvest. Fish and game had been plentiful, too. It looked like the colony would survive another winter.

The colony's new governor was William Bradford. Bradford was pleased with things. He decided to have a feast to celebrate. The Pilgrims invited Squanto to the feast because they were grateful for his help. They also invited Massasoit.

THE HARVEST FEAST

The day of the feast, Massasoit, along with ninety Wampanoag men, arrived at the colony. They brought food to share with everyone there. The Wampanoag even brought five deer to eat.

No one knows the exact date of the feast, but it was probably in the middle of October. No one knows exactly what was served at this celebration either. However, Governor Bradford had sent four men out to hunt for the feast. It is likely that they brought back wild turkeys, geese, ducks, partridges, and even swans. If fish was also served, they might have had eels, cod, bass, herring, and bluefish. Other seafood at the feast might have been clams, mussels, and lobster.

With fall came the harvest, and it was a good one. The Pilgrims felt proud of all they had accomplished in their new home. They invited the Wampanoag to join them.

Vegetables were also available. There were peas, beans, pumpkins, and other types of squash. There were also cranberries but no cranberry sauce.

Cakes, cookies, and pies were not served either. The Pilgrims had no flour left to bake with. So the Pilgrims might have made a boiled pumpkin pudding. They also had dried berries.

The feast lasted for three days. People mostly ate outdoors at long tables. There was not a building large enough to fit everyone inside.

However, there was more to this celebration than eating. The Wampanoags and Pilgrims also played games. They held footraces. The Pilgrims showed off their skill with muskets. They shot at targets. The Wampanoags did the same with bows and arrows.

THE CELEBRATION'S SIGNIFICANCE

The Pilgrims thought of the feast as a harvest celebration and a time for giving thanks. The Pilgrims were very religious. To them, giving thanks meant doing so in prayer. Along with eating and celebrating, the Pilgrims also gave thanks to God for the harvest.

As the years passed, the celebration took on a different meaning. People came to think of it as the first Thanksgiving. Yet that was not what it was for the Pilgrims and Wampanoag. It was just a time to feast and have fun.

THANKSGIVING TODAY

The first Thanksgiving was a celebration of a triumphant harvest. But the Pilgrims faced many hardships in the years ahead. At times, the harvests did not provide enough food. Later on, there was trouble between the settlers and the Narragansett and Massachuset Indians. Yet, in time, more settlers arrived and the colony grew.

The Pilgrims made a lasting home for themselves in North America. These men and women would not be forgotten. They would come to be known as the European founders of New England. Students across the country still learn about them today.

People still like the idea of the Pilgrim's thanksgiving feast. In 1941, Congress officially made Thanksgiving a federal holiday. For most Americans, it continues to be a wonderful day filled with family, friends, and feasting.

Today, Americans still celebrate the meal shared by the Pilgrims and Wampanoag. Although the food is different, Thanksgiving remains a day to spend with friends and family.

EXPLORE THE FACTS

THE MACY'S PARADE

The Macy's parade is a long-standing Thanksgiving tradition. People line the streets of New York City and watch on TV as balloons float high above the streets. The Pilgrims would surely be surprised to see that!

CHAPTER ELEVEN

WHAT CAME LATER?

The people who were involved in the harvest feast that we call the first Thanksgiving were an accomplished group. Many went on to do important things. William Bradford served as the governor of Plymouth for more than thirty years. Much of what we know about the colony comes from his writings. Bradford died in 1657.

Massasoit signed a peace treaty with the Pilgrims and never broke the agreement. He remained a friend to the Pilgrims until his death in 1661.

Though Squanto helped the Pilgrims, he also soon betrayed them. He told different American Indian groups that only he could stop the Pilgrims from attacking them. In return for doing so, these groups gave Squanto valuable gifts. But some of them also became very angry at the Pilgrims. Squanto died in 1622.

Massasoit and his warriors enjoyed peaceful relations with the Pilgrims for fifty years. However, the relationship between the Wampanoag and the Europeans would eventually change.

Captain Miles Standish led the Plymouth colony's small military force. He trained the men to defend themselves against the Narragansett and Massachuset Indians. Standish later helped start the Massachusetts town of Duxbury. He died in 1656.

As the years passed, increasing numbers of Europeans arrived and settled on the Wampanoag's land. Massasoit's son, Metacomet, became leader of his people. He was called

King Philip by the Europeans. Metacomet soon waged war on the Europeans for taking the Wampanoag's land. The two sides fought in what became known as King Philip's War. This fighting, as well as much disease brought by the Europeans, killed many Wampanoag. However, a small group of Wampanoag Indians still lives in the area. Some continue to celebrate their people's traditional festivals.

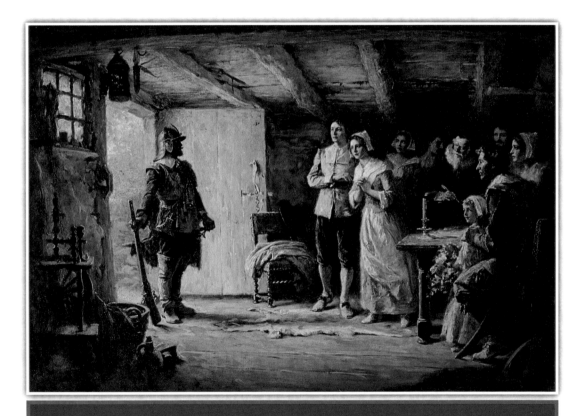

Miles Standish continued to help lead Plymouth from a military standpoint, with varying degrees of success. Eventually, he sought a quieter life and founded the town of Duxbury.

TIMELINE

1620

September 6—The *Mayflower* sets sail for North America.

November 9—Land is spotted by those on the *Mayflower*.

November 11—The Mayflower Compact is completed and signed.

December 8—"The First Encounter" between the Pilgrims and the American Indians takes place.

December 11—The exploring party selects Plymouth as the site for their colony.

December 16—All the *Mayflower* passengers arrive at Plymouth.

1621

March 16—Samoset comes to Plymouth.

March 22—Samoset brings Squanto to meet the Pilgrims.

March 23—Massasoit signs a peace treaty with the Pilgrims.

March 31—Nearly half of the settlers at Plymouth have died.

April 5—The *Mayflower* sets sail for England.

Mid-October—The Pilgrims host a harvest celebration that later becomes known as the first Thanksgiving.

1622

December—Squanto becomes ill and dies while serving as a guide for the Pilgrims. At the time, they were exploring various parts of Cape Cod.

1941

The US Congress officially makes Thanksgiving Day a federal holiday.

GLOSSARY

FERTILIZER—A substance applied to fields to make crops grow better.

MAGGOTS—The wormlike creatures that hatch from fly eggs.

MOLDY—Being covered with a furry fungus that grows on old food.

MUSKET—An old-fashioned gun with a long barrel.

MUSSEL—A type of shellfish.

PALISADE—A barrier built for protection.

PELT—An animal skin with the fur still on it.

PILGRIM—A person taking a religious journey.

SAVAGES—People who are thought to be uncivilized.

SCURVY—A disease that is caused by a lack of Vitamin C.

SMALLPOX—A serious disease that gave its victims high fevers and blisters.

TREATY—A formal agreement between two groups of people.

TYPHUS—A disease spread by insects that caused high fever and a rash.

VESSEL—A ship or large boat.

WIGWAM—Dome-topped huts where many American Indians, including the Wampanoag, lived.

FURTHER READING

Arenstam, Peter, John Kemp, Catherine O'Neill Grace, et al. *Mayflower 1620: A New Look at a Pilgrim Voyage.* Washington, DC: National Geographic, 2013.

Barber, Nicola. *Who Journeyed on the Mayflower?* Chicago: Heinemann Library, 2014.

Connors, Kathleen. *The First Thanksgiving.* New York: Gareth Stevens Publishing, 2014.

Dash, Meredith. *Thanksgiving.* Minneapolis: Abdo Kids, 2014.

Holub, Joan and Lauren Mortimer. *What Was the First Thanksgiving?* New York: Grosset & Dunlap, 2013.

Rajczak, Kristen. *The Mayflower Compact.* New York: Gareth Stevens Publishing, 2014.

Rajczak, Michael. *Life on the Mayflower.* New York: Gareth Stevens Publishing, 2014.

Stanley, Joseph. *Wampanoag.* New York: PowerKids Press, 2015.

FOR MORE INFORMATION

GENERAL SOCIETY OF MAYFLOWER DESCENDANTS

www.themayflowersociety.org

This website is sponsored by the descendants of the Pilgrims who sailed on the *Mayflower* in 1620. There is a lot of interesting information about life in the new colony.

PILGRIM HALL MUSEUM

www.pilgrimhallmuseum.org

Pilgrim Hall Museum's website has many interesting links about the Pilgrims' experience and Thanksgiving.

PLIMOTH PLANTATION

www.plimoth.org

Visit the website of a "living" museum that explores the history of Plymouth colony. Do not miss the great photos here.

INDEX